Feel-Good Spaces:

A Guide to Decorating Your Home

For

Body, Mind, and Spirit

By

Sherry Burton Ways

Wealthy Sistas Publishing House
Washington, DC

Photo by Kea Taylor

ISBN: 978-0-9833806-4-1

Sherry Burton Ways

P.O. Box 31499
Washington, DC 20030
1-800-478-0472
Email: info@myfeelgoodspaces.com
http://www.myfeelgoodspaces.com

Limits of Liability and Disclaimer of Warranty

Foreword

Margo DeGange, M.Ed.

In all of my interactions, travels, communications and adventures, I've never met a single person who didn't love the thought of having a welcoming and inspiring place to call home! No matter how much fun, hard work, or success we experience out in the world in a single day or week, we just can't wait to come home, and we want our homes to be extraordinarily special.

This book is about *Feel-Good Spaces*. It is an insightful body of work that comes from the heart of a design professional so in tune with herself, her work, and the gift her work is to others, that there is no way these words could not have been written. *We need this message.* We need to fully comprehend how important our interior spaces are to our overall well-being.

Feel-Good Spaces are more than homes or offices dressed to the nines. A feel-good space nourishes our soul and spirit. A feel good space helps us connect with others. A feel-good space supports our creativity and honors who we are at our core. This is the kind of space you dream about having and may need help creating, and I believe that Sherry Burton Ways is absolutely the woman to show you the way!

My work as a success coach and lifestyle designer involves knowing what makes people feel good, what makes them come alive, what triggers their creativity and connectedness, and what causes them to embrace peace and tranquility.

I had the privilege of getting to know Sherry when she went through my Certified Interior Environment Coaching (CIEC) program a few years back. The course focus was on helping clients create Ideal Interior Environments that are functional and beautiful, but more importantly, that supported them emotionally, spiritually, and intellectually, and fostered their personal growth both inside and outside of the home. Sherry is a natural!

I have trained many interior designers, color consultants, organizers, wellness professionals, and life coaches, but Sherry stood out to me. She knows intuitively that an exceptional interior environment is more about how it makes people feel than how it looks, even though aesthetics certainly are important.

Her entire philosophy about the home and design is rooted in an understanding that a home is an extension of the soul, and that in home-design what people are really seeking is peace, joy, balance, and beauty on a deeper plane. In my heart, I know that this (along with her exceptional technical training and skill) is what makes Sherry a stellar design expert, and it is what drives her to continually grow in her profession and use her skills to help individuals reveal their very best lives.

Sherry understands your need for an interior that will honor you and align with your deepest and truest self.

A feel-good space is something you attend to every day, because it is about "being" and "allowing", not "doing." It is about aligning with the energy that resonates with you, and allowing everything in your environment to reflect that good energy.

Get ready to take this exciting journey with my delightful friend, Sherry, as your knowledgeable and skillful interior design coach.

May *Feel-Good Spaces* continually energize and enrich you.

Margo DeGange, M.Ed.

Success Coach & Lifestyle Designer,
Creator of the *Certified Interior Environment Coaching Program* and founder of *Women of Splendor*

Dedication

For both my parents who gave me the world and provided me with opportunities to become who I am.

For my husband, Howard, who believed in me and created a nurturing and supportive environment for me to become who I am and continue to be. I appreciate your quiet encouragement and presence in our home even when I was working. Your presence kept me going on days that I did not want to. I love you always.

To my beloved twin sister, Sharon, who has been with me "40-some years and 9 months in the womb" and to my brother, Jonathan—Thank you for supporting my efforts to move forward with this book.

For those students who participated in my first interior decorating classes at the DC Department of Recreation and Dwellings in Washington, DC—You are my inspiration.

To my ancestors on both sides of my family— the Stone's, Simmons', Vass's and Burton's. To my aunts, uncles, and grandparents who have transitioned on—Thank you for giving me protection and light.

To my Spiritual Angels—Thank you for reminding me that I have all that I need to ensure that my dreams come true.

To my Spirit Guides—Thank you for helping me objectively learn from my past, treat everyone and every situation with love and kindness so as to not repeat the same mistakes.

To Almighty God, Maker of Heaven and Earth, I dedicate this work to your constant presence and source in my life.

In Appreciation

To my design colleague and friend Robin Lennon. You whipped me into shape and kept me focused. Your advice, coaching and contributions to this work will never be forgotten. Thank you.

Special thank you to my friend Margo DeGange for graciously, without question agreeing to write a wonderful forward for my book and being an enthusiastic champion of my mission.

Great thanks to color guru extraordinaire, Leatrice Eiseman, for agreeing to write the awesome testimonial for the sleeve jacket. I am honored and thankful for your friendship.

Acknowledgements

Those Who Graciously Participated in the Book:

Colette McKie, Terra Vinson, Candice Camille, Kimberly Wilson, and Jeannette Jordan

Those whose works and contributions inspired me:

Iyanla Vanzant, Dr. Wayne Dyer, Marianne Williamson, and Sanaya Roman.

My Publisher and Editor:

C. Lamar Powell, Deborah Hardnett and Wealthy Sistas Publishing House

My Photographers:

Omar Rafik, Kea Taylor, Andrew Harnik

About The Author

In 2004, Sherry Ways began to transform her life from a high powered national policy expert with the Federal Government to one that transforms people's lives through their homes. At the time, she was traveling the country and world promoting national policy in the area of transportation. Unfulfilled with her career and searching to uncover her suppressed artistic talent, Sherry began her journey in understanding herself and her knack for decorating her personal spaces. Sherry went back to school to study interior design and expanded her personal awareness through her Feng Shui studies and certification.

In 2004, she started her business Kreative Ways & Solutions, LLC, a firm dedicated to helping people create customized living and working spaces that overcome decorating challenges and evoke a feeling of well being. As the Principal and CEO of Kreative Ways & Solutions, LLC, Sherry is a Certified Feng Shui Redesigner, Certified Interior Environment Coach, Interior Color Therapist, and Reiki healer who designs soul-satisfying spaces. Sherry's work focuses on designing interiors that promote health and well being for both residential and commercial clientele. She is enthusiastic about designing interiors using color therapy, Feng Shui, and Eco-friendly design. She assists her clients in understanding what is blocking them in their lives by looking at the spaces they occupy and the colors they surround themselves with.

Currently, she lives with her husband Howard W. Ways, III and their beloved cat "Paka" in a feel-good space in Washington, DC.

CONTENTS

Preface

I recall a time in my life when I worked at a very stressful job at a small engineering firm. I was a transportation planner—a discipline in the career field of urban planning, related to the profession of civil engineering. Sounds technical right? Transportation Planners are responsible for planning the transportation system in your town, city, or locale. This field is historically male-dominated.

In the mid to late 1990's, the Clinton Administration and Congress, poured an unprecedented amount of funding into transportation infrastructure and planning in the landmark Intermodal Surface Transportation Efficiency Act or ISTEA legislation. This legislation brought a large number of job opportunities and projects in transportation all over the United States.

As a transportation planner, I worked with civil engineers in a company where the bottom line was their highest priority. In addition, I found the work environment hostile to women and particularly minorities, since there were so few of either who worked at the company. I felt no peace at work and many times I took this feeling home with me. At that time being a new wife and starting a new career, I felt disconnected with myself. I was also emotionally depressed due to the fact that in the early months of 1998, I had lost two powerful women in my life, my mother and my mother-in-law (yes, my mother-in-law), who were both influential in my life and transitioned within several months of each other due to cancer.

With this circumstance weighing on me heavily, I also felt extreme frustration working in a new industry, transportation planning, that I knew little about even with a Masters degree in hand. I graduated from my Master's in City and Regional planning at a time when ISTEA legislation was in motion and employment in the transportation field was plentiful. I was probably the first black professional woman hired in the firm's 100-year history. During this experience, I encountered every negative thing you can in a work environment—racism, sexism, being told I was not up for the job, and discouraging my contributions of ideas in the workplace as "stupid." My supervisor obviously felt uncomfortable around African

Americans and women in particular. I understood in his previous job he had few or no minorities working for him and perhaps in this new position, he had to bring in minorities to ensure certain contracts continued for the firm.

As a result, I felt an emptiness, loneliness, and extreme frustration and anger every day at my work situation. When I came home, I wanted to feel nurtured, protected, safe, and comfortable—exactly what I didn't feel at work. Intuitively, I knew I desperately needed to create spaces in my home that reflected my true self in order to keep me sane every day.

Around this time, my husband and I purchased our first home. Boy was I excited to have my own home that I could decorate the way I wanted! It needed a lot of work and love to transform it into a space that was truly our own.

With my husband's blessing and support, I had an opportunity to renovate my home in a way that spoke to me. I threw myself into this project with a passion that I had never experienced in my life before…almost as if it was a lifeline for me. I needed to empower myself and create a space that my husband and I felt viscerally fed and nourished by.

I knew nothing about color psychology, interior design principles, or interior decorating. All I knew was what I learned from scouring decorating books and studying photographs of different kinds of interior spaces. I was willing to be bold and make mistakes. I began to feel and sense my design style. I used fabrics, colors, and furniture styles that I loved. Then, to the best of my ability, I created a space that I felt really good in—a space that looked, felt and smelled like me and empowered me every time I entered it. Empowered? Yes, that is an unusual word to use in describing an interior space. And yes, your space can empower you too no matter what your circumstance, resources, or decorating savvy.

I was inspired by my African roots and created a home using colors and décor inspired by the continent of Africa. Africa is such a vast continent rich in vibrancy of color from various indigenous tribes and countries as well as the natural physical environment. I visited there twice in my life time, once to Kenya and again to Benin. Both countries were very rich in culture, textiles, and color, which inspire my design aesthetic to this day.

While in Kenya I had the once-in-a-lifetime opportunity to go on Safari and was able to get up close and personal with the richness of the African landscape. I saw the beautiful green grasslands, the powerful red clothing of the Masai tribesmen guarding their herds, the colors of the animals such as zebras, tigers and beautiful pink flamingos against the natural lakes. All these colors against a beautiful blue sky were enough to create a personal craving for this tropical feeling in my personal environment.

In Benin, I loved the beautiful fabrics worn by the indigenous people, the bright colors of flowers, natural landscapes and the food.

First, I got a picture in my mind as to what I wanted to create and determined that everything I purchased must fit into that vision, so it all flowed together harmoniously. I hunted down every African home décor store from Washington, DC to Philadelphia, to find unique masks, textiles and furniture accent pieces to acquire for my home.

I did not *clutter* my home with African objects and décor accessories. I used these items sparingly as I was determined not to over-crowd my space and over-decorate. I wanted to create something special in a Zen surface principle way.

I painted my walls a neutral shade of beige, with one wall painted in a rich red as an accent. I believe a neutral is any color that showcases the furniture, accents, and accessories. I like to surround my designs with a neutral that enables unique interior items to take center stage. I used the colors of red, yellow, a neutral taupe and blues. These various colors were used as accents throughout my home. However you may opt to use faux or a textured look that has a rough, sandy texture to create a more indigenous look.

My furniture was my own and was not new, but I accented it

with pillows made from rich African fabrics with tribal patterns. These are very appealing when accented as a throw over a sofa or stretched as a wall hanging. I purchased beautiful African carvings and masks. I incorporated my husband's miniature Asante stool and allowed it to be a centerpiece where the visitor's eye was drawn. One of my favorite items to decorate with is woven African baskets, which I used to add color and texture and used sparingly to accent my living room and kitchen areas. The touch of color and texture brought the motherland home to me in a significant way. The result was that the motherland décor nourished my spirit and my soul.

An African-inspired yellow in my bedroom with iridescent red and orange draperies, stimulated and instilled in me positive, cheerful, energetic feelings about my work situation when I awoke every day. The color red, which I used as an accent in my living room and dining room, encouraged me to cultivate my power and security. I needed to cultivate power within myself and feel secure in a situation that was not feeding me spirituality. The color orange, used in my kitchen and accents throughout my home, fueled my inner joy, excitement, creativity, movement and ambition to move forward despite obstacles in my career.

As I began my personal journey in creating my own feel-good space, my friends and family would react to my new home, and ask me why I put this color together with that color, or where I had picked up this or that piece. I felt so strong and empowered by all the positive feedback that I decided to take classes in interior design. I considered that my entire professional self-identity should shift. I felt elated.

Concurrently, I was a member of a spiritual community that encouraged learning about metaphysics, universal law, and living holistically. I was reading New Thought authors such as Iyanla Vanzant, Dr. Wayne Dyer, Marianne Williamson and others. I was learning how to manage my life, not from a point of being reactionary, but from a point of living peacefully and abundantly.

I was introduced to the ancient Chinese practice of arrangement called Feng Shui (pronounced fung shway). In addition, I began taking numerous courses both in Interior Design and Feng Shui to broaden and expand my professional foundation.

I was always very drawn to color. Color is so essential in evoking a feeling. I wanted to know about the healing aspects of color and how I could use it therapeutically while creating interiors for my clients. I learned from well-known color experts how to utilize and maximize the healing qualities of color, and I began to combine this knowledge with interior design and Feng Shui to create spaces for my clients they had never imagined. Now through this book, I want to share some of my secrets with you so you can create your own feel-good space.

To make this book user friendly, informative, and fun, I have combined exercises, my experiences working with clients, and research to help you visualize what you may want in your own space. You really can create your very own feel-good space whether it is in your home, office or both.

You may not consider yourself a creative person, but you do know when you feel good, and when you're in a space that is inviting and nurturing for you. Combine that with the progressive theories and ancient systems in this book, and you are on your way to making your space more organic, intuitive, and comforting for you, and to all others who enter it.

Everybody's Feel-Good Space will be different, but they will all have that "home" feeling, a feeling of warmth and acceptance, for the person who inhabits it. It will provide a relaxing moment in time that takes the person back to themselves elevate their mood and empowers them for the rest of their life.

Namaste!

Sherry Burton Ways

Introduction

Photo: Copyright Dreamtime

Welcome to Feel-Good Spaces! I am happy to have you join me on your journey to learning how to create a feel-good space that will delight you for years to come. I am glad to have this opportunity to join with you to take a step on your path to create a physical environment that will bring joy, peace, and love within you.

Two respected spiritual mediums, suggested that I write this book, a manual, to help others discover how their homes or offices can be a catalyst to their spiritual growth, health, and healing. Through this book, my goal is to help you expand your potential to live a satisfying life through creating an interior that reflects you, your values, and lifestyle.

Please note—not all concepts discussed in the book will be something you can relate to. As my husband often says to me when I attend a lecture, read a book, or am in any process of absorbing information, "Take what you think is valuable or the 'meat' of it, and throw away what you consider the 'bones' or things that may be non-relevant to you."

Because I have studied metaphysics, Feng Shui, Reiki, and other Eastern spiritual healing philosophies, I tend to write from this perspective. Because of my own African heritage, I have also taken liberties to provide information from an African perspective as well. I feel that this is a perspective that is not often discussed in the books about design psychology and healing. However, no matter what your spirituality or religious practice, feel free to substitute words and/or concepts that are meaningful to you.

WHAT IS A FEEL GOOD SPACE?

This is one of the easiest yet hardest questions to answer. We are asking our rooms to evoke a feeling for us. We all want that "aha" feeling when we walk into a room, but how do we get it? What exactly is it? Why is it that we feel a certain way in different environments versus others?

Several years ago, I was working with a client who was about to retire from a high-level position in the Federal Government. One of the things she consistently said to me was "I want my home to 'feel good' when I enter." As she was planning for her retirement, she wanted a completely designed home that would greet her, inspire her, and love her each and every day. Believe it or not, that was the first time I ever heard anyone describe an interior that way. The terms, "feel-good" stuck with me ever since and thus is the inspiration for the formulation of this book.

I like celebrity designer Kelli Ellis's definition of a feel-good space:

"A place where you feel transformed, energized, and productive."

What does it take then to feel transformed, energized, and productive in a space?

This book is written to help you decorate your favorite space to respond to that gut feeling, that "aha" feeling. Never mind the interior design trends found on television, written in magazines or blogs, this is about creating a decorating style that feels good to you and your family.

EXERCISES

The exercises in this book offer some suggestions on how to experience and manifest the transformation of your home interior as a feel-good space.

I have included various exercises at the end of some of the chapters to help reinforce the concepts presented to create that feel-good space you desire. The use of exercises helps to reinforce the tenants of the chapters, and provides hands-on application of the chapter subjects. I have found while teaching many classes, workshops and courses throughout my years in this business, that solid application of a topic helps to reinforce the lesson. I challenge you to use the exercises as an extension of your learning. Choose which exercises make sense to you and apply them as you see fit.

SUGGESTIONS ON HOW TO USE THIS GUIDE

Maybe you feel a need to make your home more nurturing and supportive because of other circumstances in your life. Perhaps you are newly divorced, an empty nester, or purchasing your first home and want to reflect change, growth, and progression in your space. Or you are just tired of spaces that look like everyone else's and want to reflect a style that is purely your own? You may want to attract more friends, a significant other, make a career change, or create a healthy, more satisfying life for yourself. This book may help you identify your life's ambitions, goals and passions as well show you how to reflect these in your home's interior.

There are many ways you can use this book to help you create that feel-good space in your home or office. There is no right or wrong way to use it.

Some of you may read the book straight through, chapter by chapter including working through the exercises. Others may read it from beginning to end and then go back to the exercises. Many of you may use it as inspiration when working with a decorator or designer you have hired to assist you in designing your feel good space. Lastly, you may simply begin to read a little of the book, put it down, then pick it up later when you are ready to move forward with the exercises and creating your space.

Whatever you decide, feel free to read and share it with others. Purchase a copy for a friend. Perhaps use it as an additional guide to your own spiritual journey whatever that may be.

Chapter 1
Feeling Your Desired Space

"I want a space where magic happens in every room."

~Design Client

Photo courtesy of Candice Camille, Madly Living

WHY IS IT IMPORTANT TO FEEL GOOD?

Why is it important to feel good? Feeling good makes us healthier people. Studies show that people with stronger positive emotions have lower levels of chemicals associated with stress. Also, by adopting a positive attitude people may even be able to undo some of the physical or health damage caused by everyday stress. Recent research by Cornell University Professor, Anthony Ong, PhD, provides evidence that feeling good can indeed be tied to overall improved health, as well as reduced levels of stress, pain, and illness.

His research on positive attitudes and emotions confirms that feeling good can prove to be a powerful prevention against the most common factors that decrease quality of life.

Through feeling good about ourselves and our environments, we can commune with the world on a level that empowers us as individuals to accomplish so much in our lives.

Empowerment comes from within, however, our interior environments help us manifest our hopes, dreams, and aspirations. It also alters our moods as well. In his book, *Excuses Begone!*, Dr. Wayne W. Dyer, internationally known speaker and spiritual guru, discusses how you can become empowered by your environment.

Here is Dyer's take:

> *"Make your home a temple of kindness and love. Further reinforce your new way of being by having your surroundings reflect the design of what you want your life to look like."*

Within the pages of his inspirational book, *Excuses Begone!*, Dr. Dyer reveals how to change the self-defeating thinking patterns that have prevented you from living at the highest levels of success, happiness, and health. So, as Dr. Dyer challenges you to be stronger and to become aware of your surroundings as a tool to becoming the best person you can be, I challenge you to become aware of your five senses and how they can help you create a personal space where you feel really good.

EXERCISE #1: ASSESSING WHAT MAKES YOU FEEL GOOD

What makes you feel good all over? It is a very big question. I am asking you what things make you happy on a very deep level? Whatever it is, feeling good is something we are all entitled to experience each and every day.

This is a gift we can give to ourselves. Imagine—your feel-good experience can be created and incorporated into your interior space permanently.

Begin with a journal and a good writing pen. We are going to embark on a journey to create our feel-good space. We will begin by recording our thoughts and feelings about spaces and our preferences. These tools will provide you with a personal resource that you can refer to as you create your new space. Take a moment to really *be* with your emotions and examine what makes you happy or unhappy. Answering these questions might help you.

A) List five things that make you feel-good. Be free with your answers. Don't over think it.

B) How do you escape the everyday? How do you de-stress? For example, many people jog, meditate, pray, exercise, do crafts... Whatever it is for you, make a list.

C) What are your favorite places? These could be a Vacation spot, a favorite park, a museum, or a restaurant. Maybe it is a friend or relative's home, or a spa that you like. It could be your own backyard! List three of them.

D) List at least six characteristics these places have in common that make them special to you. You might find it easier to start by listing six for each one and finding the commonalities.

Write the answers in your feel-good file or journal. We will revisit these later.

THE FIVE SENSES AND SPACE

Part of feeling good is something we experience through our five senses. What we see, hear, smell, taste, and feel in our interior environment has a huge impact on our experience. In her book, Total Design, internationally acclaimed designer Clodaugh, describes interiors and the five senses in this way:

> "Designing a living space well means celebrating all the senses and the intellect. You also want your living space to tempt and tantalize as well as challenge you to fully enjoy its sensuality."

Your interior is a manifestation of you! Your body, mind, and spirit are stimulated by all five senses—seeing, hearing, smelling, tasting and touching. Utilize them to inspire your home or office.

What are the possibilities of integrating the five senses into your feel-good space? We simply need to look around us and tap into our intuitive impulses regarding what we love and connect with, and then create what we want to see, taste, hear, smell, and feel.

Let's connect our spaces to the five senses!

Smelling

I decorated this living room using candles, which provide great fragrance for my client's feel-good space.
Photo Credit: Kea Taylor

Smell is an important sense, particularly as we create feel-good spaces. It is the second sense we encounter when we enter a space. Therefore, the smell of a space can make our experience in a room either joyful or unpleasant. There are several ways to create pleasant smells in the home. First is to burn soy organic candles. There are many on the market today and a variety to choose from. I particularly love the smell of lavender. It soothes the spirit and calms the nerves. Another is burning incense. I absolutely love the burning of good incense in my home. It tends to last a long time, even hours after, if you are entertaining friends. It is also a helpful aid in meditation and seeking clarity. There are also the totally natural potpourris that you may use to create a pleasant scent in your space.

Touching

In a feel-good space, touch can be accomplished by bringing various textures into your space. This could be accomplished by adding fabrics with strong textures—rough or smooth. You can do the same by adding wonderful area rugs that are either rough or smooth, or some place in between. Different fabrics provide different sensory experiences. For example, velvet pillows provide a sensual texture, dimension, and contrast to any area.

Seeing

Our visionary senses are the first senses we use whenever we enter a space. Therefore, they are the most important when discussing the feel and aesthetics of a space. A splash of color to any room will not only liven it up but create the mood and personality of the space. It instantly draws us in and determines whether or not the experience we will have in the space will be joyous or negative. In Chapter 5 we will explore the power of color in full detail. However, colors certainly can create and change a mood in a space. All color on the walls, artwork, accessories, furniture, window treatments, flooring, and lighting adds a specific dimension to space.

Hearing

What we hear can move us to feel good or not feel good. What we really want to hear in our sacred spaces are soothing calming sounds like music, wind chimes, running water from a beautiful fountain, etc. Consider the placement of wind chimes near doors or open windows to encourage the positive vibrations of the sounds they make as the wind hits them. I love music! All kinds of music, however, can enhance the mood of any interior space. Whether it is classical, jazz, or meditative, it will set the mood for the home upon arrival. Lastly, who can forget the soothing sounds of a wonderful water fountain that can either be placed on a wall on a special table, or on the floor?

Tasting

© *Melissa Jill Hester | Dreamstime.com*

Placing fresh fruit in a decorative bowl on the kitchen countertop or table is a fantastic way to stimulate the sense of taste. In addition, there are deodorizers, scented candles and other aroma products that contain the scents of cinnamon, baked apple pie, peaches and other citrus fruits. These can be used to bring in the feeling of taste and smells into a space.

Exploring the five senses can create a peaceful and serene atmosphere that will enhance the mind, body, and spirit. Becoming more connected to the surroundings of the home and your feel-good space, not only will become more satisfying, but inviting and relaxing as well.

CASE STUDY: CREATING A FIVE-SENSES FEEL-GOOD SPACE

A few years ago, I worked on a new home for a very special client. This was one of my first projects as a designer. Looking back now, it was my first project where it entailed me creating a feel-good space that encompassed the five senses (I did not know it at the time). First, I de-cluttered her entire home and categorized her belongings as to whether they should stay or go. I carefully worked with her to determine the significance of various items. I categorized her belongings and placed aside those items that would remain versus which ones would go.

Then I worked with the client to determine what colors were considered peaceful to her. The client stated that she liked earth tone colors. Earth tone colors are wonderful colors to place in the home because these are the colors we see most often in our natural environment. The colors, brown and a neutral color in the taupe family, were chosen. So I decorated the living and dining room of the townhome with a theme of a tropical inspired oasis. Brown is considered a stabilizing and grounding color. It was used as a color to accent her dining room which connected to her living room. The neutral taupe color was used to complete the space.

A feel-good space I created for a client several years ago
incorporating the five senses.
Photo Credit: Kea Taylor

In the living room, I worked with the client's own furnishings and accented existing furniture pieces with naturally inspired bamboo pillows and a natural jute rug. These items provide texture or the feel of the space. I added a tropical inspired accent lamp (chosen based on the client's love for travel to tropical locales), aromatherapy candles for her coffee table, and decorated with the client's own personal artwork and memorabilia. For the window treatment, rather than to purchase off-the-shelf draperies or have custom window treatments done, I accented the client's sliding glass door with sheer brown and beige colored fabric draped around it to frame it. This was done because the client loved the outdoor space in her backyard and wanted that feeling to come into the interior.

Plants and nature always have a calming effect in both work and living spaces. Because of the client's big sliding glass door, which opened, into a personal patio oasis of nature including plants and trees, I took advantage of the natural environment in her backyard, by placing the client's plants around the living area to take advantage of the light coming in from the sliding glass door. Next, to create a calming and peaceful space, I added a floor-mounted water fountain. The sounds of the water fountain and the feel of it created a calming yet peaceful space the client was after. The aromatherapy candles in the space created an intimate sacred feeling that provided a wonderful aroma for all who enter.

During the process the client stated: *"I absolutely love the way the place is coming together. My investment club thinks my home is awesome. They describe it as warm, intimate, and peaceful. Working with you has been one of the best decisions I have ever made."*

After reflecting on this project, I just realized what I gift I had to create something special. I created a space that made someone's life much more peaceful.

EXERCISE #2: DISCOVERING YOUR FIVE SENSES OF SPACE

Photo Courtesy of Dreamtime

Think about your ideal interior from the perspective of the five senses. Take a look at the suggestions below for ideas about what you prefer for each sense. Use any or all in each section, and add as many as you like. Record these in your journal.

HEAR: What sounds do you like to hear? Birds, water, the ocean, wind, music? What kinds of music? Jazz, classical, etc?

SEE: What do you like to look at? What colors are soothing to you? What shapes appeal to you? Nature, animals, wood, photographs, artwork?

FEEL: What textures and surfaces feel-good against your skin? Soft, hard, rough, smooth, wet, dry?

SMELL: What aromas are comforting to you?

TASTE: What tastes do you enjoy? Coffee, roasted peanuts, fruit, spicy food, sweets, salty pretzels, pungent foods?

Our tactile senses determine how we feel emotionally in a space. So, sensing and acknowledging what is sumptuous to us is essential in creating a space that is satisfying for us sensually.

Chapter 2
Identifying Your Feel-Good Space

"Space is the breath of art."

~Frank Lloyd Wright, Architect

A space I designed for a model home. Totally a Zen feeling
Photo Credit: Omar Rafik

One of our basic first needs is shelter. Without shelter how do we grow? How do live as humans? Studies show that even those among us who live in public housing need to feel a connection to their spaces. The meaning of home evokes a lot of feelings and emotions for different people. Beyond our homes meeting our basic needs, space in and of itself in any home is considered a luxury and we want our spaces to support us. You can redesign your entire space or designate special areas to create what you desire.

BEFORE YOU GET STARTED

Even before you start your journey to discovering your feel-good space, I encourage my clients to do a couple of things. The first thing is to think back to your childhood and determine what you liked or did not like about your home. Do you remember the color of nana's couch, whether it had plastic on it or not? Do you recall the style of the draperies in your mother's house? Consciously or subconsciously, you determined whether, as an adult, you would embrace their decorating styles or create your own.

WHICH SPACE SHOULD YOU SELECT?

A feel good space I created for a client on a rooftop deck inspired by the continent of Africa.
Photo Credit: Kea Taylor

A research study by Clemons, Searing and Temblay entitled *Perceptions of Sense of Self through Interiors of Homes*, found that homeowners tend to select rooms that reflect a sense of self, based upon whether or not they feel comfortable with the interior environmental aspects of a space and whether or not certain symbolic objects were contained within it. Typical examples would be a prayer or meditation room.

The research further states that homeowners interviewed for the study, selected spaces that represented a sense of self-worth, based on whether or not the space supported their enjoyment of favorite activities. Sunrooms in particular were noted by the researchers as a space where many enjoy reading the newspaper or a great novel.

Others stated that rooms connected to nature as the surrounding environment was a space. This could include meditation gardens or outdoor spaces. One couple in the study stated that they enjoyed fine restaurants and aesthetically pleasing environments. Therefore they felt their dining room reflected that, and their personal love for that activity.

For this book, I interviewed Yogi Kimberly Wilson, about her selection of a feel-good space in her home:

"I wanted a sweet space to accommodate my many interests and uses, crafting healing, working, living. I began with the idea of "Rock n Roll Princess" now it is more "Granny Chic Princess."

Yoga Guru, Kimberly Wilson's living room in her one bedroom condo in Washington, DC.
Photo Credit: Omar Rafik

Whatever your desire, start with the room that most intuitively meets your need to create a feel-good space.

Recently, I worked with a client who has a growing financial services practice. She worked at home quite a bit and wanted to create a special home office space that spoke to her in a spiritual way:

"I needed space in my home to focus on client cases and also feel like a sanctuary for me to be by myself and meditate and be inspired. I wanted everything in the space to speak warmth, comfort and total tranquility. I wanted to enter the space and exhale with love.

With the help of Sherry, I was inspired to create this space because I sometimes work from home and needed a quiet space away from the family to work. We already had an office in the basement, but I did not like the idea of being in the basement without a window because I felt claustrophobic."

Feel-good spaces can be home-offices like this one I designed with a warm and grounding color palette with simplistic designed furnishings.
Photo Credit: Omar Rafik

We created a color palette for the walls she liked that was inspired by a piece of artwork she had. We discussed ways to de-clutter the space (which we will discuss in the next chapter), designed appropriate window treatments, and selected very sophisticated yet feminine office furniture to fit in to the space.

She was very pleased with the results:

"I feel totally at peace and safe. I would recommend that anyone interested in creating a feel-good space go into it with an open mind and trust their instincts and heart. One should get clear on what feeling they want the room to hold for them."

This client also stated that the positioning of the furnishings and design even increased her wealth two-fold. So a very well designed feel-good space can increase your pocket book as well.

To assist you in your quest to find your feel-good space, I invite you to identify the spaces or rooms in your home where you spend the most time. Identify these spaces, and choose which ones you would like to create as personal feel-good spaces. There is no best choice for a feel-good space regarding the kind of room that is in your home. Any room in your home could be a candidate for a feel-good space. My feel-good space is a place where you can sit, read, relax, meditate, watch television, listen to music, or entertain guests. Yours may be a place where you eat, sleep, create, write, or simply dream. Perhaps your ideal feel-good space functions differently. First decide how you would like the space to function for you and then select which space will best suit your feel-good space needs.

EXERCISE # 3: TAKE A TOUR OF YOUR HOME AND REFLECT

I find it helpful to identify feel-good spaces by taking an objective tour of your home. As you walk through your home, mentally reflect on what concerns you most about specific spaces. Carry your journal and a pen with you and make notes. Don't over think this process. Make believe that you are touring your house for the first time and you are making a wish list of things you would do to improve your home in a way that makes you totally feel good. Keep your mind clear and open.

Start with the room the bothers you the most. Determine what it is about that room that needs to change in order for you to feel empowered. During this process assess your emotions about furniture, objects, room arrangement and colors in each room. Don't forget to tour your bathroom as well. Write down what words come to you about the rooms and the objects in it.

Go back to your journal that you created in Chapter 1 to find your list of your Five Senses. Begin brainstorming ways to bring those into the space you have chosen as your feel-good space. List those ways in your journal.

Recently, I was working with a client to design a brand new home for her. It was her first home, newly constructed and she was extremely excited about it. It was literally empty with the exception of a few essentials, as she had lived basically out of her suitcase for several years, living with family and friends. As we moved to design her space, I asked her to put together her vision for her new home. Specifically, I asked her to create a Feel-Good Space Inspiration Board for her home design. This board provided her a road map, a wish list, a desired action plan all in one. It helped her to focus on those things that were most important to her for the overall home design. The result was great! I took that information and created a design plan around it. She was thrilled with the results because she took ownership of it from her own vision. Based on this experience, I will provide you with the key information you need to create your own feel-good space.

EXERCISE #4: CREATE A FEEL-GOOD SPACES INSPIRATION BOARD

A Feel-Good Space Inspiration Board created by one of my clients.
Photo Credit: Author

Once you have identified a space that you would like to start with, create a Feel-Good Space Inspiration Board for that space. Find a comfortable, quiet area where you will not be disturbed. Make sure you have plenty of room in which you can spread out.

1) Gather the following:
   Travel and leisure magazines
   Home design magazines
   Blog articles online with photos
   Personal photographs
   Favorite words
   Poster board, any size
   Glue/Tape
   Scissors
   Magic Markers
   File Folder
   Your 5 Senses List

2) At the top of your board, write

   [Your Name] Feel-Good Space Inspiration Board

3) Look for words in books, magazines, or online that describe how you would like the space to feel. Cut them out.

4) Go through your magazines. Cut out photos and words you like or that feel good to you. Look at your 5-Senses List and find photos that represent them. Place put them in a special file and title it "Feel Good Inspirations." It could be a room, a color, an animal, nature etc. Do the same with your personal photographs. Once you have completed compiling your photographs, put these items aside.

5) Take out your poster board. Take the photos and words and begin to organize these items on your board. Create a collage on your poster board of words, pictures, and colors that resonate with you. Glue everything down.

Now you have your Feel-Good Space Inspiration Board. Now add your favorite scent to your completed creation board (mine is the scent of lavender) as well as textures that you like- (i.e. cotton, velvet, leather, etc.)

In Chapter 3, you will use your Feel-Good Space Inspiration Board as a guide to decorating your feel-good space.

Chapter 3
Create a Clean & Clutter Free Space

"The more you have, the more you are occupied. The less you have, the more free you are."
~Mother Teresa

Above: a clear and uncluttered living space I helped design for a model home.
Photo Credit: Kea Taylor

CLUTTER AND ENERGY

Imagine entering a space filled with clutter and objects everywhere. Think about how you would feel in this space. Nobody likes the feeling of being blocked or having things that are rushing out at you.

Feng Shui is a 6,000 year old Chinese art of placement to enhance good energy. The term Feng Shui literally means "wind" and "water". A big portion of this ancient art is "chi" sometimes called "qui." Chi or positive energy cannot flow when it is severely restricted. To the Chinese, Chi (sometimes written as "qui") is life-force energy. It is that invisible flow of air that creates good energy in a space.

To the Indian culture, the life-force energy is called Vastu which is identified as pure subtle energy that underlies all life.

In the African culture, the Ancient Egyptians also had a keen knowledge of energy forces. To create chi energy pathways they would construct walls in specific places and entrance ways. They reasoned through their architecture and design, chi energy could be enhanced and flow throughout the space.

HOW DOES LIFE-FORCE ENERGY WORK?

Here is an example of how life-force energy works. Imagine a beam of light circulating in your space. As this light circulates it beams a feel good energy that permeates the entire space. Imagine it flowing from the entrance of the space throughout an entire room. Watch as it freely moves, dips, and dives around furniture, lighting, and objects in a room that is clean, neat, orderly and uncluttered. The light moves brisk and freely while lightening the mood of the room and all who occupy it.

Now imagine that same beam of light trying to flow in a space that is full of clutter, trash, and objects with no meaning, in corners where junk and other things are placed. The light gets stuck—unable to move to permeate the space. It sits where the first clutter-mound is found and stays there unable to move. It eventually dies there with its light dimmed, unable to create good energy. This is how Chi functions in a cluttered in environment.

LIFE EVENTS AND CLUTTER

A death, divorce, separation, loss, move, or marriage may cause disarray in our lives. This can seriously affect how we decorate our personal spaces.

CASE STUDY: DE-CLUTTERING AFTER DEATH

A few years ago, I worked with a client who has recently lost her husband. She had to downsize her living arrangements from a large home in the suburbs to a two-bedroom condo in an urban environment. One of the first things we did together was to work through her anxiety of getting rid of things she no longer needed, particularly things her husband owned or had given her. We discussed this intensely because it was to be understood that in order for her new space to take form and identity, she needed to let go of the past and reshape a space that was entirely her own.

We went through an exercise in which she had to identify things that were no longer of use to her or that made her linger in the memory of her late husband. Through my direct coaching and encouragement as well as providing her categories of how she viewed the extra items in her condo, she eventually was able to rid herself of many things that linked her to the memories of her late husband. As a result, she began to feel freer, peaceful and appreciated her new condo redesign.

WHY A CLEAN AND CLUTTER FREE ENVIRONMENT IS ESSENTIAL

It is time to clear the space—physically, emotionally and spiritually. In other words, if any of your belongings add dead weight, they will create negative energy that does not belong in your new feel-good space. A clean and clutter-free environment is essential in creating a space where you feel good in.

Getting rid of physical clutter is quite possible if you really put your mind to it. Sure, many of us have emotional or sentimental attachment to certain items but the bottom line is this—if it doesn't have an obvious function, or doesn't add to your space in a positive way, get rid of it!

Karen Kingston wrote a great book called *Clear Your Clutter with Feng Shui*, where she explains clutter this way:

1. Things you do not use or love

2. Things that are untidy or disorganized

3. Too many things in too small a space

4. Anything unfinished

OBJECTS NOT USED, UNLOVED OR NOT FUNCTIONAL

Objects that are appreciated, loved, and used have strong and vital energy in and around them. Compare this to an object that is unloved, broken, or never used. What are the feelings associated with that object? Guilt, fear, obligation sadness, anger, regrets? It is necessary to surround yourself with objects you love.

You need to release the past in order to move forward and to feel good in your space.

EFFECTS OF CLUTTER

Here are some common effects of clutter:

- Ties us to unfinished projects as well as unproductive negative self talk.
- You feel stressed when you constantly see a to-do list as you look at the clutter in your rooms.
- You feel disorganized and un-centered
- Creates embarrassment
- Limits your joyfulness and sense of peace
- Creates chaos in your life
- Can create depression for you and your family
- You feel physically and emotionally heavy and overwhelmed
- Can cause you to have excess body weight
- Makes it difficult to breathe freely

-     Makes you feel exhausted
-     Keeps you emotionally bound to the past

When you begin to rid yourself of unnecessary clutter you open yourself and your life up in many ways. For example, when I de-clutter my office, I have noticed a new client may come my way or a wondrous new opportunity.

EXERCISE #5: DE-CLUTTERING TO FEEL GOOD

Find some empty boxes. Label them in the following manner:

Things I LOVE AND NEED TO LIVE AND FUNCTION

Things I DO NOT LOVE AND DO NOT NEED ANY MORE

Things I AM UNSURE ABOUT OR AM NOSTALGIC ABOUT

As you begin to de-clutter categorize your belongings in the three areas above. Place them in the appropriate box. Feel-good spaces should have only things that you love. However, be clear about whether or not they will function well in your space. Be honest with yourself. If they do not, you don't need them or want them anymore.

There will be things that you do not love that you are willing to part with. Immediately place them in your DO NOT LOVE AND DO NOT NEED Box. Schedule within two days to take these items to Goodwill, Salvation Army or any other charity in which these items could be put to better use to fulfill a need for a family in crisis.

Then there is the I AM UNSURE ABOUT OR NOSTALGIC category. These are those items that have some value to you personally. However, you may find they are not necessarily functional for your feel-good space.

Be brave. It is a hard decision to give up something that means so much to you. Meditate on it. Begin to see the true value. If it does not provide a real function to you and your life consider the following:

Step 1: Release and Cherish- Release your item so that it can start to feel like it can be a valued item for someone else.

Step 2: Visualize the Future- Envision your future in your space without the item. State affirmations of what the future will be without the item.

Step 3: Create a Ceremony of Appreciation- Find a creative way to thank your item for the memories, love and appreciation it brought you. Then send it love as you go about eliminating it from your space.

To go through the de-cluttering process, take time over the course of a week, tackling each area of your proposed feel-good spaces. Attempting a full-fledged clearing of your space all at once could be overwhelming and too emotional.

For each section of your feel-good space, begin to see it in the clearest possible light. Please I do caution you that while clearing clutter there will be emotions that will surface that you may not be quite prepared for. You may come across sentimental mementos from old partners, treasured gifts from passed loved ones or other items that might push your buttons.

By de-cluttering your space don't just consider "functional" clutter, but "emotional" clutter as well.

De-cluttering is one of the most challenging and difficult processes to undertake. Why? For some, it is a time factor and for others they wrestle with determining what to keep and what to give or throw away.

Physical clutter is linked to emotional clutter, depression, and various other kinds of negative habits and patterns.

If a space is holding past negative energy, anyone who enters that space will most likely be adversely affected by that energy on a subliminal level. This usually manifests itself in a bad "vibe" that is felt but often unexplained.

So here is your new chance to create a wide open space where you feel good and create new possibilities for yourself and your life. Your home is the physical and emotional base for you and your family and how it looks directly affects your emotional and psychological well-being.

Chapter 4
Setting the Intention

"Our intention creates our reality."
~Dr. Wayne Dyer, Author, Speaker

Photo Credit: Dreamstime

One of the most powerful things you can do to recreate your space is one of the most important to set your intention for. We set intentions for the direction of our lives by way of New Year's Resolutions. You can make a resolution for your interior space. I will now show you how you can begin to manifest your dreams into your home reality.

WHAT IS THE INTENTION OF YOUR SPACE?

Think of it this way...

Before bringing visitors into your home for a formal function, what do you do? You spruce up your home, right? You may dust off the good china, fragrance your rooms, put decorative towels in the bathroom, etc. By doing these simple things, what are you saying to your company? You are saying that you want them to feel loved and appreciated, you have set the intention.

Setting the intention is not just about the function of the room but also about the feeling and emotion that the space exudes. Setting the intention is about programming the space to provide what it is that you want it to provide.

When you take the time to 'set the intention' of a space you bring a subconscious "peace" to an ordinarily routine activity or practice. Mary Dennis, past President of International Feng Shui Guild, describes succinctly how to set your intent:

"When you are setting a space with intention, the clearing of clutter, invoking of spirit, music, incense, candle-lighting, favorite prayer, mantra, or mudra may be helpful. All these actions begin to move the energy and prepare the space. Focus on what you need to remedy in the area, and begin to set up your symbols with intent. We know that all things hold energy, so what you are intending with the placement of furniture or accessories will silently, subliminally give you back the message you set to it."

When setting the intention of your space think of yourself as an esteemed visitor. How do you wish to feel when you're in the space? This means that you must first have a clear idea of your intention and what you want.

Take your kitchen, for example. Think about how you feel when you walk into a clean, well-equipped kitchen as opposed to an unclean, under-equipped kitchen. The clean, well-equipped kitchen makes you want to prepare a gourmet meal, while the latter kitchen will only encourage you to heat up a TV-dinner in the microwave.

Your intention should be to create a space that brings out the very best in you. Your intention for your space is to feel good when you enter and experience it.

CASE STUDIES ON PROGRAMMING INTENTION

A few years ago, I went through an intention exercise with my clients who wanted a Feng Shui design of their home. Before we moved forward I scheduled an intention ceremony using the directions of Feng Shui Bagua. I took a sage stick, burned it and I, along with my clients, began by walking a specific Feng Shui pattern taught to me by wise sages and stopping at each area of the pattern in the home that guided their lives. We spoke aloud several times a special affirmation that I developed for them at each gua of the Bagua until we were done outlining the pattern. It was an amazing experience. The couple had two dogs, one of which was handicapped, both of which followed the couple through the entire process. Everyone was involved. By the time we completed, the space felt lighter and totally different. The ceremony got us all on the same page about the intention of the space, which was to create a home that feels inviting to friends and serves as an oasis to the couple.

One of my clients recently separated from her husband. She needed to set up another space that she could call her home.

Inside this client's home is a living room that speaks to her healing process from a recent marriage separation. Note the neutral colors, accessories and beautiful area rug that ground the space.

Photo Credit: Omar Rafik

This is how she described her intention for her new home:

"My specific goal for my space was to create an environment of peace, and harmony that reflects gratitude. This home represents a new start for me and an opportunity to create a space with a new appreciation for who I am and the things I have been through. I understand that the size of a home does not dictate its comfort level. It is the love within it. I grew up in very small spaces, but people always seemed to feel welcome in them. New beginnings have a high level of uncertainty and can incite a level of anxiety and fear. However, I decided to approach this new phase of my life with optimism. A new beginning inspired me to create the space I have. I learned a lot during my marriage and take those lessons forward. Among those lessons was a new sense of appreciation for home. My intent for every place that I have resided in was to make it a place of refuge. My home is a critical tool in my healing."

BRINGING INTENTION TO YOUR SPACE

So, what do you need to do to bring intentionality to your spaces?

You will need to introduce items that are both relevant and flattering to the particular space. In other words, you must look for function and appeal. Not only must the items fulfill the function for which they are designed, but they should also fulfill YOU and cater to your inner quiescence and well-being.

In working with my clients there are various rituals and activities that I use to help them program their space. But now I will introduce you to some basic principles to help you reveal the intention of your space.

EXERCISE #6: SETTING THE INTENTION

Before you determine the intention for your feel-good space, take some time to ask yourself the following questions:

1.) What is the purpose for this space?
2.) How do I want to feel when I enter this space?
3.) What is it that I would like the focal point to be in this space? In other words, is there an architectural feature such as a fireplace, a large window, or artwork that should be the center of attention.

Then, take time to meditate and pray about what it is that your space is intended for. Clear your mind of any negative thoughts or feelings. Make sure that you clean your space thoroughly. De-clutter if necessary.

Next, ask yourself, "How do I want to feel when I enter this space?" Go back to your Feel Good space Inspiration board that you created in the previous chapter. Look at it, meditate on it, and use it to program your intention for the space.

The words that you collected on your vision board can assist you in creating a powerful affirmation for the space.

List all the things you would like for your interior to say, do and feel for you and your family. Then start setting about implementing it, one week at a time.

Make an affirmation of what your end-goal or desire is to be for your feel good space. State it in the present tense. Here is an example:

"I affirm that my feel-good space is an oasis for inspiration, for laughter, music, art, and good chi for all who enter."

See how that was formulated? When you formulate an affirmation it automatically programs you and the energy of the space.

When you affirm whatever you desire for the space make sure it is stated in the present tense, not the past, or the future. The goal is to ensure that the space is programmed for the present as if it already happened.

Once you have completed this portion of the intention setting, take a piece of sage that you can burn and walk around the room repeating your intention of the space. Sage is an ancient space-clearing tool used by Native Americans and others to clear negative energy in a space. You can purchase sage sticks through organic food stores or herbal shops in your community.

Through this exercise you are not only programming or setting intention for the space but you are also clearing the space as well. Wave the sage stick around the room. Be very thorough here... Make sure that you enter every corner and cover all the empty spaces within the room. Chant your affirmation at least seven times in each corner of the room. Lastly, come to the middle of the room and close your eyes and simply state "And So It Is, Amen" or whatever comes to mind to close out your intention.

Remember—your emotions and thoughts have power over your space. If you have a space that invokes negative feelings when you enter it, then you have lost intentionality and the space will never make you feel good or serve its purpose.

Chapter 5
Your Empowerment Colors

"Pay attention to your feelings. Don't be concerned with what others think. Color is a highly personal choice."
~Leatrice Eiseman, Color Expert

© *Gina Smith* / *Dreamstime.com*

THE IMPORTANCE OF COLOR

When it comes to color everyone has a very different opinion as well as a strong preference. Therefore, color is a powerful tool and should be used carefully in our feel-good interiors.

The colors you choose should say things about you: who you are, what you wish to express, what you need, what creates the environment that you desire. This is why, when you are moving into a new home or thinking of redecorating any space you already have, it is the perfect time to evaluate how to create a feel good space that brings out the best in you.

Our first impressions and reactions to color are most often rooted in our childhood experiences. Our most memorable reactions to color are from happy, sad or traumatic moments in our lives.

CULTURAL COLORS AND MEANINGS

© Djembe / Dreamstime.com

Regardless of your ethnic background, how you view color can be based on where you were raised and different aspects of your culture. Here are a few examples:

Yellow, in Asian cultures, is considered sacred or imperial. In Western cultures, it is a symbolism of joy and happiness.

Red, in China, is a symbol of celebration and good luck. In India it is considered a color of purity. In the United States, it is considered a color of Christmas Holiday and Valentine's Day. In Côte d'Ivoire & South Africa, the color symbolizes Mourning.

The color, white, represents mourning or death in Eastern cultures, while in the United States we see the color Black in that way. In Nigeria, the color symbolizes good luck or peace. In Zambia, it represents goodness, cleanliness and good luck.

The link between color-symbol and religion is obvious. In Ireland the color, orange, has a Protestant religious significance. For Hindus, Blue is the color of Krishna. In India, Green is the color of Islam.

Deep blues and reds are the most popular colors for intricate designs in South Africa, with outlines created in black and white. Red is usually reserved for ceremonies and worn by chiefs in Nigeria. Different shades of red denote different tribes. In East Africa, blue beads are thought to enhance fertility.

Color symbolism within the Akan culture of West Africa influences the colors of their widely known Kente Cloth. Colors are chosen for both their visual effect and their symbolic meanings. A weaver's choice of colors for both weft and warp designs, may be dictated either by tradition or by individual aesthetic taste. There are gender differences in color preferences, dictated by tradition, individual aesthetic taste and by spirit of the occasion.

COLOR THERAPY/PSYCHOLOGY

In the work I do for my clients' interiors, I use a concept called Color Therapy. What is Color Therapy? Simply, it is the therapeutic use of color to heal. It was originally a concept in which color and light were used to heal the sick in ancient times.

Ancient Egyptians were one of the first people that used color therapy. Of course at that time they did not have glass windows. But they would drape colored fabric over entrance ways, right where the sun shone through them. This way the sun would shine over those who needed healing from some sort of illness. As part of the healing process, the Egyptians would dress those who were sick in colored clothing in accordance to the type of condition that needed healing.

In the Hermetic tradition, the ancient Egyptians and Greeks healed with colored minerals, stones, crystals, salves and dyes and painted their sanctuaries with healing colors. The ancient Greeks used color to restore balance.

Here is a quick breakdown of the healing, therapeutic and home design aspects of our favorite colors. This could be used as a key to understanding how color can work for your feel-good space:

Color: Black

© Pisetsak | Dreamstime.com

Black is a multi-dimensional color that is associated with power, sophistication, formality, elegance, wealth, mystery, style, unity, and professionalism.

Color: Blue

Photo Credit: Dreamstime

Blue is a calming color and gender neutral. It is associated with tranquility, calmness, trust, and loyalty. Blues slow the heartbeat. They lower blood pressure, ease stress, and enable us to breathe more deeply.

Color: Brown

Brown is one of the leading colors in the earth tone family. When paired with the color, green, it is often associated with the eco-friendly and environmental movement. Brown is a grounding color that promotes a comforting feeling. Brown offers stability, tradition, wholesomeness, steadfastness, simplicity, friendliness, and dependability.

Color: Green

Green is a healing color and also a powerful representation of the eco-friendly movement. Green is also associated intelligence, nature, spring, fertility, youth, environment, wealth, and good luck.

Color: Orange

Photo Credit: Dreamstime

Orange is an energetic, enthusiastic balancing color. The color is symbolic of cheer, happiness, heat, fire, nourishment, flamboyance, playfulness, and desire.

Color: Purple

Photo Credit: Dreamstime

Purples are soothing and tranquil colors. Purple can symbolize nobility, meditation, spirituality, creativity, royalty, wisdom, enlightenment, peace, and well-being in an interior.

Color: Red

Photo Credit: Dreamstime

Red typically symbolizes passion, strength, bravery, danger, energy, fire, sex, love, romance, excitement, speed, heat, ambition, leadership, and courage.

Color: White

©Tatiana Morozova | Dreamstime.com

White is often associated with cleanliness or sterility. But it can also symbolize neutrality and peacefulness. It is the preferred neutral in most interiors.

Color: Yellow

Photo Credit: Dreamstime

Yellow evokes feelings of happiness and typically symbolizes sunlight, joy, happiness, earth, optimism, intelligence, idealism, wealth (gold), summer, hope, femininity, gladness, sociability, and friendship.

CASE STUDIES ON COLOR THERAPY

One of my first design projects almost ten years ago was creating a home based holistic healing center. This project was created for a newly established business owner who was a reiki healer and therapist. In this project, I created a home-office retreat or oasis for her and her clientele using the principles of feng shui and color therapy. I used the healing color of sage-green as the neutral or main color of the space. Sage-green was used in the space because it is associated with kindness, caring, compassion, and sharing, which was the business owner's desire that her clients feel when entering her office. Sage-green is a color that helps with matters relating to the heart. Then as an accent color I used Saddleback Brown. Browns can be a constant source of energy, making us feel supported and strong. Browns are practical and trustworthy colors, which was another key feeling my client wanted to evoke for her clients.

For this client I created a healing center using Feng Shui and color therapy.

Photo Credit: Kea Taylor

The result was phenomenal. The client stated:

"Sherry did an amazing job designing my healing center. I was extremely impressed with the finished space. My clients love my center and often comment about how wonderful they feel when they are in the space."

Another great example of decorating for healing comes from a friend and colleague, Candice Camille, Co-founder/Owner of "Private Stay at Madly Living" in Fort Washington, Maryland. She made a decision to create a bed and breakfast solely for the purpose of healing those who stayed there. Her decision to open Private Stay at Madly Living Bed and Breakfast was due to her personal battle and survival of Tracheal Cancer. These experiences led her to pursue her passion and dreams of creating the ultimate space of self-pampering in the spirit of health and wellness in the form of a Bed and Breakfast. The decor and therapeutic visualization of each room in the Bed and Breakfast was inspired by the concepts of Feng Shui, tranquility, and the feeling of peacefulness.

Turquoise and bold colors create a peaceful refuge at Madly Living Bed and Breakfast.

Photo Courtesy of Candice Camille, Madly Living.

The colors chosen for the décor of the bed and breakfast in particular take you to a wonderfully spiritual place. The design of the bed and breakfast is classic, eclectic, and includes African American and African inspired artwork and accessories that reinforce spiritual beliefs, comfort and peacefulness. Warm neutral colors accented with darker deep rich colors create a stunning effect. Warm neutrals like cream, beiges, and taupes accented by yellows, terracotta, peaches, and turquoises provide a rich and comforting backdrop to the spaces. The furniture is simple, solid dark wood pieces made from mahogany or walnut. Rustic pieces make bold accents. Luxurious fabrics such as silk and taffeta provide that extra touch to make guests feel comfortable and pampered.

The décor and color schemes for each of the guest rooms and the main areas were inspired by her African roots, the principles of Feng Shui, and the feeling of overall peacefulness. She gets a multitude of compliments from all who visit and stay at her establishment.

PERSONAL EXPLORATIONS OF COLOR

Think about how you felt as a child. What were the colors in your bedroom? Do you remember the colors of the interior spaces of your parents' home, or of your grandparents' home? Maybe of Aunts and Uncles or childhood friend's houses? If you had a negative experience in the past and you can recall an associated interior color around it, it is best not to use that color in your feel-good space.

Are there colors you are drawn to based upon cultural, religious or spiritual reasons? Answering these questions may be a start to creating a color palette that speaks to your feel-good space.

Collect paint chips and look at them together. Even if you might imagine that they "don't go together" you might find that they go surprisingly well together because of your love and appreciation for them. Make sure that you have them in your feel-good space.

Also consider a recent vacation you may have taken or a new place that you never visited before. What are your favorite vacation spots? Was one of the reasons you enjoyed it because you loved the colors of the landscape, the buildings, and the people? Why not consider including some of those colors in your feel-good space?

Your left brain is stimulated by color while your right brain is stimulated by words. There must be homeostasis in the human environment another words, from a Feng Shui perspective a Yin and Yang.

If we balance ourselves through our environments we should have the right combination of both warm and cool colors.

When I create a color scheme for a client I always create one that balances both warm and cool colors. I always select a neutral color that would permeate the majority of the wall color. A color scheme that limits you to two or three colors in one color can create a subliminal imbalance. Variety and balance of warm and cool colors brings a feeling of wholeness and connection to a space. From a Feng Shui perspective it provides both the Yin (feminine) and Yang (masculine) for the space.

FENG SHUI AND COLOR

The 6,000-plus ancient Chinese art of Feng Shui also teaches us that feel-good spaces or spaces with good chi and energy, should be composed of all the colors of the five elements.

The Chinese recognized that color has an impact upon us. Our body is about natural flow within and our world of nature has a natural flow. Acupuncturists work on the inside of the body to maintain its natural flow. The practice of Feng Shui works with the natural flow outside of the body.

Colette Mckie, an acupuncturist in Maryland, describes it this way:

Colette McKie chose colors for her acupuncture office to correspond to the five-phase correspondences to human body organs.
Photo Credit: Omar Rafik

"Acupuncture is based upon our relationship to nature. Every color has a tie to one of our organs! The Chinese perceived that our organs are the origin of our emotions. Have you ever wondered where our emotions come from? All people have the same emotion, regardless of race, creed, color, or gender. So, I knew from my training that the colors I chose (in my office) would immediately start influencing a person's body function as well as their emotions."

In Chinese acupuncture, there is a theory of the 5 phases. This theory looks at 5 interrelated forces that have specific relationships to one another. The five images or elements used to describe these forces are Wood, Fire, Earth, Metal, and Water. Each of these elements has corresponding organs, emotions, colors, tastes, tissues, and human sounds. The following table shows some of these 5-phase correspondences:

	Wood	Fire	Earth	Metal	Water
Yin Organ	Liver	Heart	Spleen	Lung	Kidney
Yang Organ	Gall Bladder	Small Intestine	Stomach	Large Intestine	Urinary Bladder
Color	Green	Red	Yellow	White	Black

When I study a client's birthdate using Chinese astrology, I determine whether or not they are missing or lacking a particular element that would help balance them in an interior. I will often incorporate just a particular color to represent a missing or displaced element to help the individual feel more balanced in their interior environment.

For a husband and wife client who purchased their first home, I developed a color scheme based on their personal feng shui readings. The husband, a Yin Wood type, needed more water, which was represented by blue, to enhance his energy.

The wife was an extreme Yang fire element. We had to cool her fire a bit by bringing in the water element.

Each of the chosen colors through their Feng Shui analysis was painted on various walls in the home including a blue accent wall. The combination of the colors of both the couples' readings are repeated in tiny rectangular tiles, arranged in a geometric pattern and mounted around the fireplace. The result is a reflective, shimmering work of art.

A living room I designed using Feng Shui and Chinese Astrology to create a customized color palette for the ceramic tiled fireplace.
Photo Credit: Andrew Harnik

The five elements according to Feng Shui are as follows:

Water- Colors: Black & Blue

Wood- Color: Green

Fire- Color: Red

Earth- Colors: Beige, Tan, Yellow

Metal- Color: White

Representation of the Five Elements. Clockwise from the top right Fire, Earth, Metal, Water, and Wood.

Here is an example of how you could use these Feng Shui colors in your space:

Photo Credit: Kea Taylor

Blue Walls, Red Accent Wall, Green Plants, Earth-tone flooring, and window treatments accented by a white ceiling and accents.

However, you don't have to use Feng Shui colors to create balance in your space. There are so many wondrous ways to use color in creating our feel-good space!

USE A COLOR WHEEL

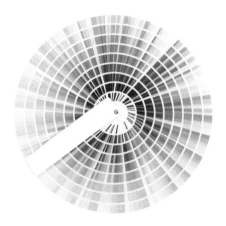

Photo Credit: Dreamstime

Color wheels can be found through various retailers, like art supply stores! Here is a quick synopsis of how to use it:

- Using three colors adjacent to each other on the wheel will create a harmonious scheme.

- Using opposite colors on the wheel creates an energy balance.

- Using three colors from three sections of the wheel are known as triadic color harmony and these are useful when creating a lively and interesting room scheme.

- Using a neutral background and combining any of the above in furnishings and objects in the room will create a comforting energy balance.

EXERCISE #7: DISCOVERING COLORS YOU LIKE.

Take a tour of our home. Browse room-by-room and pick out the colors you like to look at on your walls, fabrics, window treatments, furniture, flooring etc. Make a list of these colors under "Colors I Like." Then, pick out all of the colors that you don't like and list them under "Colors Not Preferred." Then out of the all the colors selected select those that are neutral to you. Neutrals are typically colors like beige, taupe, green, gray, etc. However, there may be other colors that you identify that appear neutral to you. Once you look at all three lists identify the top three colors you like and see if they correspond to your list of neutrals from the color wheel exercise above.

Chapter 6
Creating Comfortable
Arrangements of Furniture

"Know your lines and don't bump into the furniture."
~Spencer Tracy

© *Tim Martin* / *Dreamstime.com*

The arrangement of your furnishings is a key essential component to successfully creating a space that feels good to you. That space cannot effectively be created without carefully and thoughtfully planning the layout of the rooms of your furnishings as well as the styling and the proportions and scale of the room.

The best designed spaces are the ones that express the *being or personality* of the individual that uses it. Therefore, the furniture placement and style reflects the ideal use for the room and interpretation.

CHOOSING THE RIGHT FURNITURE

Here are some key areas to consider in choosing and arranging furniture in your feel-good space:

Always carefully measure the space which you plan on furnishing. Creating a floor plan is a must. How many times have you purchased furniture just to find that it either does not fit in the space, is not proportional to the space, or simply is not suitable for the space?

Is there a natural focal point to the room? An architectural feature such as a fireplace, a large window, or a wall feature? Make sure you note the location and size of these features on your floor plan. Your focal point does not have to be an architectural feature. It could be a favorite piece of furniture which could be a great source of inspiration for your feel-good space.

Now, some people may not know what particular decorating style they prefer. They may have an idea but may not be sure of how to express it or how to describe it. There is a simple way to get over that – buy a décor magazine at your local drugstore, bookstore or magazine shop. Research and choose the design style that you like. Buy several. Review websites to learn about the different styles of furniture that are available. There are so many design styles from contemporary/Zen to English or American Traditional and French Country. In addition, consider visiting model homes in new housing developments to get a sense of style represented. Take photos of the rooms and furnishings you like (provided you have permission).

In an interview with Yogi Kimberly Wilson, she describes her design style for her 600-square-foot condo in Washington, DC:

"My zodiac sign is cancer so home is very important to me. I need functionality mixed with spice, flair, and femininity. I've been a fan of Rachel Ashwell's Shabby Chic style for years... Yes, working within 600 square feet as a living space for five beings is no small feat. Also, shifting styles when moving to

my space was a challenge in deciding what to keep and what to let go."

Look at the photos of rooms; cut out the ones you like and those you do not like. Make notes to yourself on why some rooms appeal to you and why some do not. Make a file of those you like and study them. Look at the colors, the furniture, the accessories and the ambience created in each photo. This will help you to begin developing a decorating style that is uniquely yours.

Also, look objectively at the furnishings in other rooms of your home. You will become aware of the furniture styles you have purchased in the past and therefore, that will provide you with a clue of what you like. You may want to continue this same furniture style in your feel good space or begin to add some different new elements.

Visit a couple of local furniture stores who sell the kind of furniture that you are drawn to. This is a must! Sit in the furniture that you like. See if it is comfortable to you. Feel the textures of the upholstery and fabrics. What textures feel good to you? What does not? Feel-good space-design is about comfort and the feeling of relaxation. Pick furniture that feels good to you and is well-made with a reasonable warranty. In addition, good energy means that preferred feel-good furnishings have rounded not jagged or sharp edges. Consider round tables and curved lines when you are choosing your furniture, for the new space that you are designing for yourself and your family.

You may want to consider purchasing sustainable, environmentally friendly furnishings. This is furniture that is made out of recycled, reclaimed, and renewable materials and wood. A recent study found that the use of wood in an interior environment "can help to create healthful environments, and commonly evoked descriptors for rooms include 'warm,' 'comfortable,' 'relaxing,' 'natural,' and inviting.'"

Some authors and teachers of holistic-design state that some furniture is considered more comforting and nurturing than others. Some examples of these furniture types include: large floor cushions, large soft inviting sofas and arm chairs. However, I advocate that you select the type and style of furnishings that feel good to you.

Also, let's not forget the colors and finishes of the furniture. Are the colors complimentary (soft) or contrasting (dynamic)? Make sure you take your color swatches for your room color with you when visiting a furnishings store to make sure the colors work well together. If necessary revisit the color wheel exercise in the previous chapter to ensure that you are mixing and matching your furnishings with the appropriate color scheme for your feel-good space. Talk to the sales people at the store about fabric and color choices and whether or not your fabric colors need to be customized.

Once you have purchased your furniture, based on your measurements, try grouping your furniture into conversation areas or vignettes (no more than 12 ft. square). Determine if the amount of seating is adequate, and consider angling your furniture if necessary. Check in with feelings about the room. Does it feel good to you? If it doesn't, shift your furniture around until you feel intuitively that it meets your definition of a feel-good space. Do you need more seating, less seating? Adjust as necessary.

One thing I would caution you about is lining up your furniture against the walls in your space. It does not add interest and creates a less than creative and feel-good flow to the room. Also, consider finding an area rug to help to group furniture in interesting ways and *ground* the space. It also provides color and an accent for the room.

Lastly, a feel-good space is a balanced space so consider the following:

1) Your walking space between furniture should be no less than 24-36 inches wide.
2) If you create conversational areas with your furnishings, 8 feet is the maximum distance between seating.
3) No furniture should be in front of door openings that would inhibit walking or traffic flow.
4) Eliminate all unnecessary clutter.

Remember the principles of design to always consider: balance, harmony, rhythm, focus, contrast, and proportion to create a great feel-good space.

EASTERN PHILOSOPHIES OF FURNITURE ARRANGEMENT

Vastu Shastra is the age old Indian science of design and architecture of the built environment. It is what I call the Indian version of the Chinese Feng Shui. 'Vastu' essentially means 'dwelling' in Sanskrit. Vastu primarily focuses on the spiritual, psychological and physical aspects of the interiors and buildings taking under consideration the energies of the cosmos. This practice is heavily weighed on how the solar system affects residents and influences the built environment. There are specific rules for healthy and holistic methods of constructing homes.

Some of the most important Vastu principles are as follows:

-The living and dining rooms of the home should be located in the north-east, north-west, south, or west directions.
- Furthermore, furniture in those rooms should be positioned in the south or west directions.

Feng Shui principles around furniture arrangement tend to center on ensuring that the arrangement does not evoke negative energy circulation.

From a Feng Shui perspective, create arrangements that provide you full command of the room when seated. In other words, arrange the main seating so that you can clearly see all who enter and leave the space. This Feng Shui universal principle is known as the "Command Position." Also avoid placing large or main pieces of furniture directly opposite the entrance to the room which therefore, becomes vulnerable to all the energy that enters it.

CURVED VERSUS RECTINGULAR FURNISHINGS

Photo Credit: Dreamstime

As mentioned earlier in this chapter, one of the things I do when I select furniture for my clients is to select furniture that is curved or that has rounded edges. This is because the chi flow of a room moves better around furniture that is round versus furniture that is square. Overall my clients give me high marks on their overall feeling of a room when I employ this approach to selecting and arranging furniture.

Sha energy is the opposite of Chi energy. In Feng Shui, sha energy is considered negative or unhealthy energy. The concept of the poison arrow is a sha energy field that is associated with sharp objects and corners. If you have sharp objects or corners such as found in rectangular furniture, it may impact you negatively if you are sitting in its pathway.

Dazkir and Read in their research *Furniture Forms and Their Influence on Our Emotional Responses toward Interior Environments* support the fact that curvilinear furniture is better for feel-good spaces. In their study, 111 participants were evaluated and interviewed on their preferences of furniture forms. In their study, "curvilinear forms" elicited more pleasant emotions than did rectilinear forms (of furniture). In addition, respondents preferred to spend more time in rooms that had curved furniture design because the "furniture looked more comfortable, interesting, and calming compared with the rectilinear furniture." The study concluded that "pleasant-arousing emotional states such as feeling pleased, peaceful, contented, calm, and relaxed" were associated with furniture with curved designs.

If you already have existing furniture in your chosen feel-good space, I would encourage you to consider the principles and advice above to ensure that your space and the furniture arrangement creates that relaxed feeling you are seeking.

Chapter 7
Empowering Your Space with Personal Objects

"Always surround yourself with things you absolutely love."
~Sherry Burton Ways

Photo Credit: Candice Camille, Madly Living

PRSONALIZING YOUR SPACE

No matter what circumstances we find ourselves in, we have control and authorship over our interior spaces. At home, we can exercise authority by personalizing our space in some way. Personalizing a space feeds one's spirit. It can define our inspiration. It can be anything that feeds your spirit in a positive and energizing way.

Photo Credit: Omar Rafik

I find it more important than ever to feed my spirit in the place I reside. Be it temporary or permanent, a home should be a place of refuge. So I have been inspired to create my living space as a refuge with many things that I find beautiful.

Your personal gifts can inspire your feel-good space. Be it the rug for your living room or a candle someone gave you as a part of a special holiday or birthday gift. Your rug could contain all of the colors you wear frequently and to which you clearly have a natural affinity. A candle can inspire accent pieces for a single room.

From a more practical standpoint, everything in your feel-good space does not have to match. Just select things you love. The things you love may be from a store, your travels (e.g., a rock from a beach), posters from concerts, pictures from life events, gifts, etc. It is important to know that just because a store sells a set of matching furniture does not necessitate   you to buy the set. I will make the analogy of bananas in a supermarket: Yes, there may be ten bananas in the cluster, but you only need or want five. So you break apart the bunch and walk away with five. There is no crime in taking only what you want. You know best what works in your space.

You want to have things that you really truly treasure around you in your space. Feel-good spaces always have beautiful and special decorative items and mementos that have deep meaning for you—things that bring you joy!

One of the main tenants of feng shui is to surround yourself with things you love. It could be a piece of lace, a nicely framed photograph, a favorite armchair, an autographed book, a nice piece of artwork, or a bouquet of fresh flowers. These are the niceties that make a feel-good space a space to be loved and cherished. In addition, it builds and creates any space with a story, memory, and a sense of personal history.

A client's sorority photo, fresh flowers and a replica of a favorite shoe created a personalized sitting area created in her condo.

Photo Credit: Kea Taylor

Placed thoughtfully and strategically, your very favorite items and cherished decorations will be just the finishing touches you need to complete your feel good space. However, remember that these items cannot be cluttered. They should be placed in your space in such a way that they create and promote conversation.

For example consider tastefully representing personal photographs custom-matted and framed with nice black or white frames in white mats (or in colored or wooden frames) that are consistent and placed strategically along an important and coveted wall in the home. Make your own mini-gallery. This is a wonderful way to tastefully represent memories in a decorative way in the home. I had a client who wanted to display photos of her children for a basement redesign project. We found some great frames at a discount store and *viola*; we created her personal beach-themed gallery, showing beautifully photographed children playing, while on a family vacation, at the ocean in her children's playroom.

A client tastefully created a photo collage with identical framed photographs with white mats to decorate a family centered feel-good space.
Photo Credit: Omar Rafik

ART AND YOUR FEEL-GOOD SPACE

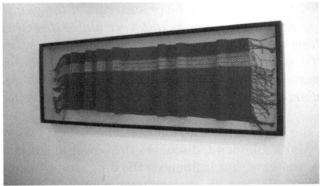

A client treasured her fabric from Indonesia and I framed it to create a centerpiece in her hallway.
Photo Credit: Author

I love artwork! I think that artwork in a space creates an energy about it, a finishing touch. It is in my opinion one of the most important accessories in a feel good space. When I think of art I don't just consider fine art on the wall, but photographs, sculpture, art dolls and other decorative objects.

Our artwork:
- Is a reflection of who we are as individuals
- How we few others and their cultures
- Has an influence on how we behave and feel
- Provides a snapshot from others of our identity.

In Feng Shui everything contains energy; even artwork. Pay attention to the subject matter of art hanging in a gallery, museum or a store. What is the artist conveying in the art piece? Does it speak to you? What about the colors of the artwork? How does the piece make you feel? Authors, Vincent M. Smith and Barbara Lyons Stewart, in their book, *Feng Shui: A Practical Guide for Architects and Designers,* discuss the energy of artwork in this way:

"One of the most important Feng Shui concepts to remember in choosing art is that the emotions and feelings of the artist go onto the canvas or into the object in the creative process. However, the process does not stop there. Those same emotions reflect back at us every time we look at the art. If the artist was angry when he or she created the painting, we will experience that anger as if it were aimed directly at us every time we look at the picture and every time we merely enter the space in which the piece of art can affect our subconscious. It is critical to be aware of the emotions that a piece of art generates before selecting it for a particular spot."

Also in the popular book and movie, The Secret, Feng Shui Master Marie Diamond, discusses the power of the subject in artwork and how that influences the feng shui of a space. She counseled one of her clients who were a single bachelor interested in finding love and getting married. However, throughout his home were paintings of single women looking away or appearing uninterested in him when gazed upon.

Diamond suggested he paint artwork that showed a happy couple who appeared interested in each other. He did just that and within a year was happily married to a wonderful mate.

CULTURALLY SIGNIFICANT SCULPTURES AND ANTIQUES

Many of us have treasured objects including antiques that have been passed down to us from our families and loved ones. These objects can certainly create a wonderful addition to your feel good space. However, I must warn you to be careful to examine these objects closely to ensure that the energies of the individuals who had given it to you are good and wholesome and will add good chi energy to your space.

For example, say you inherited a beautiful antique vase from your grandmother. Maybe your grandmother was not the nicest person from your memory or from your family recollection. Maybe she was considered dysfunctional. Do you want that energy in your home or feel good space? Think about it.

Also, many of us travel around the world and find masks, sculptures, and other objects from exotic places like Africa, Indonesia or South America. Before you purchase or place these objects on your wall, take a look or research the history of the mask or sculpture and what it meant to the culture you are getting it from. Make sure it was for something peaceful or beneficial in the culture and thus will be for your feel-good space.

An African Shona sculpture creates an artful conversation piece in a client's outdoor space.
Photo Credit: Kea Taylor

EXERCISE #8: SELECTING PERSONAL OBJECTS THAT MAKE YOU FEEL GOOD

So now let's focus on your feel-good space. What personal objects do you want to place in your feel-good space? Let's explore.

First identify the objects, photos, artwork, etc. that you would like to place in your feel good space? List them here:

_____

_____

_____

_____

Describe what it is about the objects that makes you feel good or empowers you?

_____

_____

_____

_____

Why do you feel it is necessary and important to place them in your feel good space?

_____

_____

If you did not have the object(s) in your feel good space how would you feel?

_____

_____

_____

_____

Do you have the space for the object(s)? Will the personal object be hung on the wall or on a piece of furniture?

_____

_____

_____

_____

Will the object be secure at its location? Yes___ No___

Will the object(s) create unnecessary clutter? Yes ___ No___

Will the object coordinate as an accessory or accent with the rest of the décor? Yes___ No___

If no, would you consider placing the personal object in another space? Yes___ No___

What other things should you consider in placing the personal object in your feel-good space?

_____

_____

_____

_____

Chapter 8
Your Overall Feel-Good Space

"The ache for home lives in all of us, the safe place where
we can go as we are and not be questioned."
~Maya Angelou

Photo Credit: Candice Camille, Madly Living

While you may enjoy creating a feel-good space that is
interesting and physically attractive, make sure that you
make it about you and your life and not about your neighbors
or what other people think or approve of.

To pull it all together, I am summarizing the suggestions that
our case study participants provided me regarding things to
consider in placing the finishing touches on your feel good
space:

- Take an assessment of where you spend the
  most time in your home or office.

- Be very clear about what you want to project in your feel-good space and what you are naturally drawn to.
- Create a unique space that works with your personal lifestyle.
- Incorporate small touches that work within your budget.
- Delve into yourself to know what you love rather than what is the current trend at the time.
- Make your space easy to change. For example paint is easier to change than wallpaper.
- Use items as you decorate that have meaning to you. It always amazes me what an impact this has on a space.
- Pay close attention to what makes you feel comfortable and at home, energetic, peaceful, or creative. Surround yourself with colors and objects that will support that.
- Be conscious of the size and scale of objects you place in your space as not to overwhelm the rooms.
- Create plenty of walking space between your furniture.
- Let your feel good space intuitively speak to you to guide you where things belong.
- Select new items to compliment items that you already own.
- Ensure that all of your choices in your feel good space contribute to serenity, rest and intimacy with yourself and others.
- Be inspired to create a living space and a refuge with things that you find beautiful.
- Integrate space-saving, versatile pieces that can be easily moved or repurposed.

No matter what the size or constraints of your space; love and nurture it. This world tends to value "excess," i.e. the more/bigger, the better. I am not convinced that the economic downturn of the past few years has taught us (Americans) much.

Create your space from love. That love will be returned to you over and over again. Whether you live in 350 square feet or 10,000 square feet of living space, your feel-good space will reflect the spirit that you create in it.

It really does not matter what goes on outside of your feel-good space, you have authorship/authority over what goes on inside. Only welcome people and things into your feel-good space who appreciate you and your space. Anyone that you welcome into your space should feel privileged to be there and thus, treat your space with the utmost honor and respect.

Also, you are responsible for protecting your space against any and everything you do not want in it. Don't ever be afraid to remove anyone or anything that is disruptive to yourself or your space. After all, any source of the disruption is disturbing something you love and treasure.

Select things that are functional in places where functionality is necessary. If you love it, but it does not serve its purpose, what good is it?

Creating a feel-good space is a continuous work in progress, i.e., interactive. Your mood may change and so can your space. You may have a new need, so your space can change to reflect that need. Do whatever works best for you at the time. Stay true to yourself. The only rule is to do what makes you feel good.

Peace and blessings!

BIBLIOGRAPHY

AD. Ong. **Pathways Linking Positive Emotion and Health in Later Life**. *Current Directions in Psychological Science*, 2010; 19 (6): 358 DOI: 10.1177/0963721410388805

Clemons, Stephanie A., Searing Erin E. and Tremblay, Kenneth R. **Perception of Sense of Self Through Interiors of Homes.** Housing and Society, Volume 31, No. 2, 2004 pp 130-144.

Clodaugh, **Total Design.** Clarkson Potter Publishers, 2001

Dazkir, Sibel S. and Read, Marylin A. **Furniture Forms and Their Influences on Our Emotional Responses toward Interior Environments.** Sage Publications Environment and Behavior, 2011; DOI: 10.1177/0013916511402063.

Dennis, Mary. Course: School of Graceful Lifestyles, Mary Dennis, 2008.

Dennis, Mary. **Millennium Magic.** Feng Shui Quarterly, International Feng Shui Guild, Spring 2000.

Dyer, Wayne W. **Excuses Begone**! Hay House Publishing, 2009.

Ellis, Kelli. Design Psychology Course. NESTA, 2012

Kingston, Karen. **Clear Your Clutter with Feng Shui**. Random House, 1998.

Krishna, Talavane. **The Vastu Workbook**. Destiny Books, Rochester, Vermont, 2001.

Lenclos, Jean-Pillippe and, Lenclos, Dominique. **Colors of the World: The Geography of Color.** W.W. Norton and Company, New York, London, 1999.

Mitchell, Marlene. Course: The Magic of Color. Aromatherapy Institute.

Nofzinger, Lynne. Holistic Home Decorating Accessorize With the Five Senses
Suite101: Holistic Home Decorating: Accessorize With the Five Senses | Suite101.com
http://suite101.com/article/holistic-home-decorating-a190074#ixzz219ilD2sB

Rice, Jennifer and Kozak, Robert. **Appearance Wood Products and Psychological Well-Being.** Society of Wood Science and Technology, 2006; 38(4) pp. 644-659.

Smith, Vincent M. and Lyons Stewart, Barbara. **Feng Shui: A Practical Guide for Architects and Designers.** Kaplan AEC Education, 2006.

CPSIA information can be obtained at www.ICGtesting.com
Printed in the USA
LVOW011755061212

310448LV00004B/9/P